WHAT CHURCH
DO YOU BELONG TO?

Pastor Dominic Correlli

What Church Do You Belong To?
by Pastor Dominic Correlli

Copyright © 2018 Perry Hall Family Worship Center.
www.perryhall.life

ISBN 13: 9781731286307

Dedication

This book is dedicated to people who desire to
have a relationship with God.
It is dedicated to those who are seeking out a church built
on Jesus Christ. Allow this book to help you identify,
find and open your eyes in your search for
what church you should belong to.

Acknowledgments

None of this would be possible without God. I am grateful for His love for me, my family and the world. John 3:16 (NLT) "For God so loved the world that He gave His one and only Son, that whoever believes in Him shall not perish but have eternal life."

A very special thanks to Lisa, my loving wife, copartner in life and ministry. Thank you for all your behind-the-scenes guidance, support and encouragement; without it, this book would not be possible.

To my children and their wives, Dom Jr., Ashley, Nick, Becky, John and Christiana. Thank you for your continued support and encouragement through countless decisions in ministry and building the church. Special thanks to Christiana for all the effort and time spent on this book.

To my grandchildren: Thank you for bringing me so much joy!

To my parents: Thank you for raising me in a Godly household and teaching me right from wrong and giving me and my siblings direction in life and for life.

Thank you all for your continual love and support.

About the Author

Pastor Dominic Correlli serves as the Senior and Founding Pastor at Perry Hall Family Worship Center in Perry Hall, Maryland. Pastor Dom and his high school sweetheart, Lisa, wed in 1982. Since then, they've built a home and family. They have raised three sons into mature men who love the Lord and have wives who also love the Lord. Pastor Dom and Lisa are now proud grandparents.

Starting out working at his family roofing business, Pastor Dom felt the call to start a church in 2001. Later that year, Perry Hall Family Worship Center began meeting in their home. Thinking it would only last a few short months, nine years later in 2010, the church's home was moved to its current location. Pastor Dom and Lisa still work to create an inviting environment for the church as if they are welcoming you into their own home.

CONTENTS

Introduction

If Jesus said He would build His church, then why are there so many denominations and doctrines out there? With over thirty-five million churches in the world and over thirty-three thousand different denominations, what church do *you* belong to?

Churches branch off into other churches. Denominations branch off into other denominations. There are so many types of churches: home churches, small churches, mega-churches. Sometimes we ask ourselves the question, "Which church is the right church for me?" With all of these different denominations, churches, and doctrines, we might also ask ourselves, "Are they all the true church, or is the only genuine church the one that I belong to?"

Jesus created the original design for the church, and over time men and women formed different denominations. Human beings have a way of assuming that they can make adjustments to the original design of the church to make it better. Centuries of man's ideas being added to God's design for His church have resulted in churches that have moved away from what God originally intended. So let's rewind the tape and get a better understanding of God's design for the church by looking at His Word.

The Master Architect

Jesus, the master architect, explained His design for the church to Peter in the book of Matthew. He begins by explaining to Peter that the most important part of the church is its foundation. The foundation is what the church will be built on. In Matthew 16:18, Jesus said, "And I also say to you that you are Peter, and on this rock, I will build My church, and the gates of Hades shall not prevail against it."

In this verse, Jesus addresses Peter, which in the Greek language is translated *petros*. *Petros* means "small rock" or "pieces of rock." Jesus refers to Himself, however, as Rock, or *Petra*, meaning "a boulder or large mass." Obviously, any structure needs to be built on a large mass. In this passage in Matthew, Jesus is instructing Peter to build the church on Jesus Himself. Jesus is stating that He, as the solid rock, is the foundation on which the church should be built. The foundation is critical because the entire building is set on the strength of the foundation. The right foundation is important because it determines the strength and integrity of a structure.

The same is true for a belief system. Just like buildings and structures, our faith needs a firm foundation to support us and hold us together. As we submit to Jesus and build our faith on His foundation, He will protect us from false teachings and doctrines that may try to deviate us from the truth. When a house is built on the right foundation, it will pass tests over time. Storms may come and pound on a house, but the house with a good foundation will withstand any adversity. If our faith is built on Jesus we will be secure from false teachings and doctrines. Again, Jesus refers to himself as *Petra*, meaning "a boulder or a large mass," while speaking to Peter as *petros*, meaning "pieces of rock." Man-made religion does not have the foundation of true faith, the latter of which is built on the Lord Jesus.

Jesus makes it very clear that the church is to be built on Him and Him alone. He is the founder and architect. The church that Jesus was talking about is not the *church* as we know it today. It is not a structure or a building. Jesus calls a group of believers the church, which means "the called-out ones." This refers to the congregation or whole body of Christian believers. In Matthew, Jesus created the church and made Himself the foundation of everything on its belief system. The church is not a structure, organization or denomination. It is the body of believers.

The Church Age Began

The Church Age began when the "called-out ones" began to assemble together. Not long after that beginning, however, the church began to move away from the design that Jesus intended it to follow. Jesus makes note of the churches that began to take a different course in the book of Revelation. In the following chapters, we will look at each of the seven churches that He mentioned and discover what the Lord says about each of them.

Before we get started, we need to understand a few things about what Jesus is saying and to whom He is saying it. We will see in these verses that the Lord Jesus is talking to a group of people as well as individuals, both being considered the church.

The book of Revelation opens with the letters from Jesus to the seven churches. During the time that the apostle was exiled on the Isle of Patmos, Jesus revealed Himself to the apostle John in a vision. Jesus gave the apostle John the seven letters which are now found in the book of Revelation. These letters addressed the churches, explaining the Lord's concerns about the infiltration of unsound doctrines and practices. Jesus was basically giving the seven churches a report card. He revealed the heart of these churches and instructed them on what they needed to do to put things back on the right track.

These are seven churches that actually existed in the Roman province of Asia. Jesus addressed the churches by the name of the city in which they were located. Although they were actual physical churches in that time, there is also a spiritual significance that we as believers can take away from the letters to the churches and apply to our lives today. Jesus' message to the seven churches is still relevant for us and for the church.

Jesus' Instructions

Before Jesus begins to share His message to the churches, He helps us understand the symbolism that is being used.

"...The seven stars are the angels of the seven churches, and the seven lampstands which you saw are the seven churches" (Revelation 1:20).

The seven stars or angels that Jesus mentioned means "messenger." The lampstands are the "church." A lampstand is intended to hold light. John 8:12 says, "Then Jesus spoke to them again, saying, 'I am the light of the world. He who follows Me shall not walk in darkness, but have the light of life.'" The people of God, as individuals and in congregations, are called to be bearers of light.

> The people of God, as individuals and in congregations, are called to be bearers of light.

Before we read the Lord's concerns about the first church, we are given valuable information that helps us understand this entire study and apply it to our own lives. In Revelation 2:1, Jesus addresses the first church. He makes a comment for all these churches—as well as for the church today.

"These things says He who holds the seven stars in His right hand, who walks in the midst of the seven golden lampstands" (Revelation 2:1).

Jesus makes it clear that His presence resides within His church. There is only one church, and He is the foundation. If your church is built on Jesus Christ and He is the master, the leader and the center of your church, you should know that He is present. Remember that the group of believers that you belong to makes up the church that Jesus was talking about. Jesus writes the letters to the seven churches because they belonged to Him. As we read through the letters, we know that Jesus wrote to the churches to bring correction because of His love for them. As humans we can easily get off course if we are not maintaining a strong relationship with the Lord. Godly correction and discipline help us stay on course. At times, God gives us warnings, and it is our job to recognize them. God uses correction and discipline to help us get our lives right with Him because our eternal destination depends on it.

> If your church is built on Christ and He is the master, the leader and the center of your church, you should know that He is present.

In Matthew 7:21, Jesus says, "Not everyone who says to Me, 'Lord, Lord,' shall enter the kingdom of heaven, but he who does the will of My Father in heaven." We need to be careful that we do not make assumptions about our faith, such as assuming that we are right with God when we actually are not. Sometimes we believe that we are right about something when we are actually wrong. Sometimes we think we are being the church—but we are just being religious.

Some people live for their retirement, but God says we are to live for eternity. The decision for eternity happens here on earth. A person may know a few churchy words, pray every now and then or even be a nice person. We know through reading the Word of God that these things do not get a person into heaven. The enemy intends for us to drift away from the Lord. He uses our selfish desires, hobbies, jobs, money, business, entertainment and many other tricks to distract us and get us off course. Religion could be one of Satan's greatest distractions. It is his intent to cause us to drift away from the Lord.

The Word of God Brings Correction

The Lord warns us in 2 Timothy 4:3-4 (NLT), "For a time is coming when people will no longer listen to the sound and wholesome teaching. They will follow their own desires and will look for teachers who will tell them whatever their itching ears want to hear. They will reject the truth and chase after myths."

As you read about and evaluate the seven churches from Jesus' perspective, please allow the Word of God to bring correction into your own life. Allow the Scriptures to challenge and encourage you. Remember the Lord corrects us because of His love. His will is that no one will be separated from Him. As you read through the following pages, ask the Lord to reveal to you, "What church do you belong to?"

CHAPTER ONE

Ephesus

"To the angel of the church of Ephesus write: These things says He who holds the seven stars in His right hand, who walks in the midst of the seven golden lampstands. I know your works, your labor, your patience, and that you cannot bear those who are evil. And you have tested those who say they are apostles and are not, and have found them liars; and you have persevered and have patience, and have labored for My name's sake and have not become weary. Nevertheless I have this against you, that you have left your first love. Remember therefore from where you have fallen; repent and do the first works, or else I will come to you quickly and remove your lampstand from its place—unless you repent. But this you have, that you hate the deeds of the Nicolaitans, which I also hate. He who has an ear, let him hear what the Spirit says to the churches. To him who overcomes I will give to eat from the tree of life, which is in the midst of the Paradise of God"(Revelation 2:1-7).

We now begin with the letter to the first church, the church of Ephesus. In Revelation 2:1, Jesus was walking in the midst of this church. The seven stars represent the messengers of the churches. The messengers referred to are possibly a pastor or even a specific angel for the church. The lampstand represents the churches. However, it is important to keep in mind that Jesus is in the midst of the churches as well. Remember, these churches are built on the foundation of the Lord Jesus Christ.

In modern times many assemblies call themselves a church, yet they do not fulfill the basic requirements. A real church is one where Jesus is Lord and He and the Bible are at the center of everything. As we continue to examine the seven churches, you may notice some have veered away from that which was correct.

In verses 2 and 3, Jesus begins by complimenting the church of Ephesus.

"I know your works, your labor, your patience, and that you cannot bear those who are evil. And you have tested those who say they are apostles and are not, and have found them liars; and you have persevered and have patience, and have labored for My name's sake and have not become weary" (Revelation 2:2-3).

Verses 2 and 3 explain attributes that all churches should aspire to have. This church is doing their job. Like many churches today, the church of Ephesus has a lot going on. They are feeding the hungry, participating in mission work, hosting programs for all ages, hosting Bible studies, meeting in their homes and having prayer nights. This church did not allow evil to enter into their camp. Some churches tolerate sin, hide it or try to pretend that it does not even exist, but the church in Ephesus did not mess around with sin. This church made a point to deal with their sin immediately and remove it.

The church of Ephesus also investigated those who claimed to be godly. They would research these people to identify if they were who they said they were. This is something that all churches need to implement. When a pastor allows someone to speak in his pulpit to his people, he gives his approval to the person who is speaking. Pastors have an obligation and a responsibility to do a complete background check and to receive approval from the Lord before allowing anyone to speak to or lead within their churches.

> Pastors have a responsibility to do a "background check" and to receive approval from the Lord before allowing anyone to speak to or lead within their churches.

The church in Ephesus was not a lazy church. They were persistent and worked hard to complete church projects. This church was like a lot of other churches and even individuals; they were busy working for the Lord. What they were doing was good, but what Jesus says in verse 4 is very important.

"Nevertheless I have this against you, that you have left your first love" (Revelation 2:4).

Jesus is telling this church that they became so busy doing good things until they believed that their efforts were good enough. But Jesus says, in other words, "wait, you are missing something here."

This sounds a lot like some of us today. We think our works and our efforts will please the Lord, but He really desires for us to love Him and have a relationship with Him.

Let's put this concept into perspective. A man needs to provide for his family. Because he currently is not making enough money at his job to provide for his wife and family, he picks up a second job. At first, the increase in pay helps meet the financial needs of the home, but over time, his marriage starts to fall apart because he became distracted and left his first love. This man was busy trying to do good for his family by working more and more to provide for them. Meanwhile, he was sidetracked from his relationship with his wife. We all can get distracted by the busyness of life. Even as this could happen in a family, it can also happen in our relationships with the Lord. The devil uses busyness as a trick to divert our attention and take our eyes off the most important thing, Jesus.

QUESTION

How can we return to our first love?

Although Jesus is putting pressure on this church, He is not finished with them. He gives them a second chance to get into right standing with Him by giving them a warning.

"Remember therefore from where you have fallen; repent and do the first works, or else I will come to you quickly and remove your lampstand from its place—unless you repent" (Revelation 2:5).

Jesus reminds the church of Ephesus to get back on track by going to the starting point, the time when they first fell in love with Him. It is a very special time in our lives when we first encounter the Lord and accept Him as our Savior. When we fall in love with Him, it is a special time. There will never be another experience like it. If you have given your heart to the Lord, you understand the feeling of the first love. If you think you gave your heart to the Lord and do not recall this feeling, it is possible that you were going through an external routine and were not sincere. Take some time and ask the Lord to return you to His first love.

The demands and cares of this world will pull us away from our first love if we allow them to.

Life will continue to keep us busy. There will always be demand after demand, bill after bill, distraction after distraction. The demands and cares of this world will pull us away from our first love if we allow them to. It takes a lot of intentionality to live a balanced life. Jesus gives the church of Ephesus instructions on how to make things right and return to their first love. He gives them a stern warning and instills a sense of urgency.

Do you ever wonder why some churches close down? Could it be because they left their first love? The church probably started out on the right track but got distracted and veered off the course that was intended for them. Jesus warns the church in Ephesus to turn around and repent, or His presence would leave their church.

In verses 6 and 7, Jesus begins to wrap up His letter to this church. He started out the letter by complimenting the church, but then He shed light on their problem and gave them the solution. Now He affirms the church's hatred for the teachings of the Nicolaitans. "But this you have, that you hate the deeds of the Nicolaitans, which I also hate. "Then, Jesus makes a promise. "If you hear and obey, you will enjoy the tree of life and Paradise in heaven."

"He who has an ear, let him hear what the Spirit says to the churches. To him who overcomes I will give to eat from the tree of life, which is in the midst of the Paradise of God" (Revelation 2:6-7).

Not all denominations and churches are under the headship of Jesus Christ because some have drifted away from the essential doctrines of the Bible. When a church or a person deviates from the truth that is in the Bible, they are not a part of the church that Jesus established. Unfortunately, many churches today uphold traditions before they uphold the Word of God.

If you have accepted Jesus Christ into your heart, then you are a part of the church that Jesus created. If you are looking for a church to attend, here are some key factors to consider.

- First, Jesus must be the center of everything.

- Next, the church has to be 100 percent Bible-based. There should be no other writings that are taught above the Word of God.

- It is important to review the church's statement of faith because, most of the time, it will tell you a great deal about the core beliefs and priorities of that church.

- Also, they must believe that salvation only comes through Jesus Christ. His death on the cross and resurrection from the dead makes it possible for us to experience God's forgiveness.

God created His church for His glory. It is His will that we be part of His church. The only true church is built on the Lord Jesus. He loves His church, and we are to love it as well.

Perhaps you have drifted away from your first love of Jesus Christ, but it is not too late to fall in love with Him again. Or, maybe you never fell in love with the Lord. The last chapter of this book will guide you into the relationship that God desires to have with you.

QUESTIONS

What does it mean to love the Lord with all your heart, soul and mind? How can you practically do that today?

"And you shall love the Lord your God with all your heart, with all your soul, with all your mind, and with all your strength. This is the first commandment" (Mark 12:30).

CHAPTER TWO

Smyrna

"And to the angel of the church in Smyrna write: These things says the First and the Last, who was dead, and came to life: I know your works, tribulation, and poverty (but you are rich); and I know the blasphemy of those who say they are Jews and are not, but are a synagogue of Satan. Do not fear any of those things which you are about to suffer. Indeed, the devil is about to throw some of you into prison, that you may be tested, and you will have tribulation ten days. Be faithful until death, and I will give you the crown of life. He who has an ear, let him hear what the Spirit says to the churches. He who overcomes shall not be hurt by the second death" (Revelation 2:8-11).

The second church that Jesus writes to is the church in Smyrna. In verse 8, He makes it very clear who the author of this letter is. He says, "To the angel of the church in Smyrna write: These are the words of Him who is the First and the Last, who died and came to life again." Revelation 2:8 reiterates something that is noticeable throughout Scripture: that Jesus identifies Himself as the First and the Last. Again, in Revelation 22:13, Jesus says, "I am the Alpha and the Omega, the Beginning and the End, the First and the Last."

Many so-called "spiritual" or "religious" leaders have walked in their own ways and gathered their own followers. But each of them has died, never to be heard of again. It is documented that Jesus died on the cross and rose from the grave. Jesus is the only one who gave up His life as a sacrifice for us to pay for our sins so that we may have eternal life with Him in heaven.

After making His visit to the church, Jesus gives a report, "I know your works, tribulation, and poverty (but you are rich); and I know the blasphemy of those who say they are Jews and are not, but are a synagogue of Satan" (Revelation 2:9).

> The Lord sees us always, whether we are walking in obedience to Him or in disobedience.

When Jesus states, "I know your works," He is basically telling the church of Smyrna that they are seen. We can take this as a reminder that the Lord sees us always, whether we are walking in obedience to Him or in disobedience. He notices what we are up to. In times of temptation, He sees us. When we do something pleasing to Him, He sees it. If no one else has ever seen what we do, we can know for a fact that God sees us.

Next, Jesus points out three major things about the church of Smyrna: their works, tribulations and poverty.

There is no doubt that when someone is in poverty in the middle of a tribulation, their situation becomes even more hopeless. In this case, the church of Smyrna was exhausted by their works, dealing with poverty and in the middle of a time of tribulation. It is obvious that this church was experiencing a lot of trouble. The name Smyrna means "myrrh." Myrrh is a perfume that comes from a tree that grew in the region that this church was located in. This specific tree would release the myrrh fragrance when it was being put under pressure or being crushed. The name is fitting because the church of Smyrna was being crushed by persecution.

QUESTION

How can we build our foundation on Christ?

When you accept Jesus as Lord and Savior and become a follower of Christ, you can be called a Christian. Christians are what make up the church. To say that life would be smooth after getting saved would be to speak a lie. The Bible never said that walking with Christ would be easy. A good example of this is the parable of the two foundations found in Matthew 7:24-27. This parable is about a godly person and an ungodly person who built their houses on two different foundations. One was built on the sand, the other one was built on a solid rock. If you remember from the introduction, the solid rock represents the Lord. The storm came and hit both houses, but the one with its foundation built on the rock stood firm.

Although we may belong to a church, this does not mean that we will not experience tribulations. Jesus is talking in this passage about spiritual wealth. Spiritual wealth will always benefit us, but the problem with this church in Smyrna and possibly us is that we may be living like persons who are spiritually poor.

> Our God is a God of healing.

Jesus mentions that this church is receiving another attack, the blasphemy of the Jews. If we look at the core of the situation, the Jews were not really responsible for this church's persecution, Satan was. Regardless of the source, however, this church had a lot of adversity surrounding them.

Sometimes we feel the same way—as if the world is coming down all around us. Sometimes it feels like we are being attacked from every angle: our health, finances, relationships, family and so on. God says we have a large spiritual account that we can draw from that comes through our relationship with Him. True peace comes from the Lord.

In verse 10, Jesus brings a warning to this church that we can apply to our lives today. "Do not fear any of those things which you are about to suffer. Indeed, the devil is about to throw some of you into prison, that you may be tested, and you will have tribulation ten days. Be faithful until death, and I will give you the crown of life" (Revelation 2:10).

The Lord tells us, "Do not fear." Fear could lead to failure, but we do not have to fear because Jesus has already won all our battles. Sometimes, it may appear as if we are losing battles, but when we understand how much Jesus loves us, we win.

In this verse, "for ten days" means for a period of time. Yes, we may suffer, but only for a period of time. Then Jesus says, "Be faithful until death, and I will give you the crown of life." God does not always deliver His children from suffering and persecution, but He does promise an eternal life with Him. Many godly brothers and sisters have gone home to be with the Lord, but never received their healing here on earth. In heaven, they are not only totally healed, but they have also received a great reward which is the crown of life.

Jesus then concludes His words to the church of Smyrna by identifying the most important reason for being in right relationship with Him: "He who has an ear, let him hear what the Spirit says to the churches. He who overcomes shall not be hurt by the second death" (Revelation 2:11).

Jesus concludes by explaining that, if they will listen to Him and obey Him, they would not experience the second death. The second death is otherwise known as eternal separation from the Lord.

You may notice that Jesus did not have a strong word of correction to give to this church. He does not say that He has something against them, as He does with the other churches. The message that He is trying to convey to this church, however, is that they are not living out the fullness of what the church is intended to be. You have a spiritual bank account that you may not yet be fully tapping into. Yes, you may have experienced problems in your life, but because you are a child of God, you have the power to overcome them.

QUESTION

What does it mean to be rich in the Lord?

When we look at this church, we notice that Jesus' message to them is one of hope. Remember, in the Lord, you are rich. In the Lord, you have an eternal reward. In the Lord, you have eternal life. As we experience trials in our lives, we must keep these thoughts in front of us. We cannot allow the cares of this world to bring us down. We need to tap into the Lord's source and realize that He is for us and not against us!

Soak in that truth: He is for you, not against you. We are victorious over the trials of life through Him! 1 Peter 5:7 (NLT) says, "Give all your worries and cares to God, for He cares about you."

Let me challenge you with this: stay faithful, and do not leave your first love. Do not miss out on the spiritual blessings that the Lord provides for us. God has given us the spiritual blessings of peace, guidance, acceptance, protection and much more. We do not need to carry the unnecessary cares of this world. We do not need to live in spiritual poverty. Instead, we need to make sure that we are living in the fullness of His love by tapping into Him.

CHAPTER THREE

Pergamos

"And to the angel of the church in Pergamos write: These things says He who has the sharp two-edged sword: I know your works, and where you dwell, where Satan's throne is. And you hold fast to My name, and did not deny My faith even in the days in which Antipas was My faithful martyr, who was killed among you, where Satan dwells. But I have a few things against you, because you have there those who hold the doctrine of Balaam, who taught Balak to put a stumbling block before the children of Israel, to eat things sacrificed to idols, and to commit sexual immorality. Thus you also have those who hold the doctrine of the Nicolaitans, which thing I hate. Repent, or else I will come to you quickly and will fight against them with the sword of My mouth. He who has an ear, let him hear what the Spirit says to the churches. To him who overcomes I will give some of the hidden manna to eat. And I will give him a white stone, and on the stone a new name written which no one knows except him who receives it" Revelation 2:12-17.

Did you know that it is Satan's mission to distract believers? He will do anything to trick and deceive us. He will try to use entertainment, hobbies, our jobs and many other things to distract us. If we are not careful, he will also work his way into our churches.

> Even in an evil environment, God can still see us and is watching over us.

The next church on Jesus' list is the church of Pergamos. As always, Jesus identifies Himself as the author of this letter. As the founder of the original church, Jesus is inspecting and pushing for change where needed.

"I know your works, and where you dwell, where Satan's throne is. And you hold fast to My name, and did not deny My faith even in the days in which Antipas was My faithful martyr, who was killed among you, where Satan dwells" (Revelation 2:13).

Sometimes, children try to hide things from their parents when they know that they have done something wrong. No matter if you are a child or an adult, God sees you and knows what you are up to.

After identifying Himself as the author, Jesus tells the church of Pergamos that He knows where they live. In verse 13, Jesus says, ". . . and where you dwell, it is where Satan's throne is."

These people lived in a very pagan atmosphere and in the midst of great idolatry. Satan's operations take place all over the world, but Jesus says Pergamos was where Satan's throne was located. Some believe that this is where Satan's headquarters are. It is important to know that our enemy, the devil, is not just sitting in his office in hell with the heat turned up. He is busy working in different areas and trying to disrupt our lives. However, even in an evil environment, God can still see us and is watching over us.

Then, Jesus mentions Antipas. We do not know exactly who he was; Antipas could possibly have been the pastor in the church of Pergamos or one of the church leaders. What we do know is that he was a follower of Christ and a martyr for his faith. The fact that Jesus mentioned Antipas teaches us that a truly committed Christian has access to the power of God, even in the midst of the work of Satan.

Now in verse 14 Jesus comes in with the punch. He begins to name-drop.

"But I have a few things against you, because you have there those who hold the doctrine of Balaam, who taught Balak to put a stumbling block before the children of Israel, to eat things sacrificed to idols, and to commit sexual immorality" (Revelation 2:14).

Jesus calls out the leaders of the church who are giving false teachings. Balaam was an unrighteous prophet for hire. Balak, the King of Moab, wanted to get rid of Israel. King Balak had paid Balaam to curse Israel three times. Every time Balaam tried to curse Israel he failed, so he came up with another plan. If he could not curse them, he would try to earn his money another way—by corrupting them. His plan was to get the Moabite women to move amongst the Israelite men and intermarry. Once the Israelite men and Moabite women intermarried, the women would have great influence to pull the men away into the lifestyle of the Moabites, a life of idolatry. Balaam's plan eventually worked, and it contributed to the separation of the people from their God.

This is a great lesson for us to learn. If we do not continually stay focused on the Lord, we can be misdirected. It is up to each of us individually to keep our eyes on the Lord. We do this mostly through the reading of the Bible, praying and spending time with godly people. If we do not know the truth, we will not be able to recognize false doctrines. God warns us in many scriptures not to connect with the wrong people. If we are living a godly lifestyle and truly living for the Lord, we will know who to hang with or without. In 2 Corinthians 6:14-15 (NLT), there is a warning for believers: "Don't team up with those who are unbelievers. How can righteousness be a partner with wickedness? How can light live with darkness? What harmony can there be between Christ and the devil? How can a believer be a partner with an unbeliever?"

In the church or in our very own lives, God absolutely condemns teaming up with unbelievers and allowing them to speak into our lives.

The church in Pergamos compromised and allowed false doctrine to creep in. We all need to watch out for compromise. We cannot compromise the things of God. It is a slippery slope when we justify something that the Bible condemns. Compromise happens a lot in people's lives, as well as in the church. There is no place for sin in the leadership of the church. The church is to lead people into living a holy and devoted life by obeying the Word of God. God does not tolerate sin and neither should we as believers. When we allow ungodly television shows or dirty jokes to be a part of our lives, we put our spiritual condition into jeopardy. The evil in the world can influence us if we allow it to. The Nicolaitans influenced the believers in Pergamos in a negative way.

> We all need to watch out for compromise. We cannot compromise the things of God. It is a slippery slope when we justify something that the Bible condemns

"Thus you also have those who hold the doctrine of the Nicolaitans, which thing I hate" (Revelation 2:15).

The Nicolaitans taught Christians that it was acceptable to participate in pagan orgies, which brought immorality and idolatry into the church. They believed that what they did with their bodies did not affect their spirit. The people of the church suffered because of the poor choices that the leadership made in allowing these acts, based on pagan beliefs, to be brought into their church.

"Repent, or else I will come to you quickly and will fight against them with the sword of My mouth" (Revelation 2:16).

Jesus gives the church of Pergamos an ultimatum. They must repent and turn from their ways, or else. There is no room for compromise and toleration of any form of evil in a believer's life, nor in the church. 1 Corinthians 5:6 (NLT) explains how quickly sin spreads, "Don't you realize that this sin is like a little yeast that spreads through the whole batch of dough?" Just like yeast, a very little bit of sin will spread. There are plenty of scriptures warning believers not to dabble in sin.

"He who has an ear, let him hear what the Spirit says to the churches. To him who overcomes I will give some of the hidden manna to eat. And I will give him a white stone, and on the stone a new name written which no one knows except him who receives it" (Revelation 2:17).

God gives the church of Pergamos a promise; He tells them that, if they listen, they will hear His voice. Many people say that they do not hear from God or God doesn't speak to them. Well, He certainly does speak, but how?

The first way God speaks is through His Bible. When we read the Bible, God speaks to us through His written word. The Greek word *logos* means "written word." This is what we see on the pages of the Bible. *Logos* will tell us the past, present and future events. It tells us God's laws and His desire for us. Many historical and future events are recorded in the Bible from creation to the cross to the end times. God's written Word speaks to us.

But there is another way that God speaks to us. The Greek word *rhema* means "the spoken word," or the words that are not written in the Bible. Both words, *logos* and *rhema*, are Greek words that mean "word," but one is the written word and the other is the spoken word. As we grow in relationship with God, we will begin to hear and sense His *rhema* word.

Does God talk to us audibly? Sometimes, if He wants to, but typically most people hear His voice on the inside of them. Have you ever heard someone say, "I feel it in my gut" or "I just know it was from God?" This is the assurance that you know it was God speaking to you. This ability to discern God's voice comes as our relationship with God grows. It is like when someone very close to you calls you on the phone, maybe your spouse or children. All they have to do is start talking and you know who it is. Why? Because of the closeness you have with each other. It is the same with God; as we continue to grow closer to Him, we can learn how to recognize His voice.

But in order to hear clearly, we need to be tuned in. Years ago, in order to listen to a certain station on the radio you had to turn the dial. If you were close enough to the station, you would begin to pick up the sound, but sometimes there was also a lot of static. As you turned the dial closer to the station, the static would slowly disappear. Our lives are the same way. Our own thoughts and the distractions of the world are the static. We want to hear from God, but we have too much going on in our head. We need to turn the dial and tune into God more and more so that we can keep the static out.

> We know that God wants to hear from us—
> but God also wants us to hear from Him. We cannot hear very well if we are not focused in on Him.

We know that God wants to hear from us—but God also wants us to hear from Him. We cannot hear very well if we are not focused in on Him. When we focus or tune in, we can begin to hear God. Sometimes it is hard to identify if it is our voice, the devil's voice or God's voice speaking to us. One thing to consider is what we are hearing needs to line up with God's written Word. For example, God will not ever tell you that you do not need to forgive someone because His written Word says we need to forgive everyone. As we read His *logos* word, the written Word, to know more about His guidance and direction for our life, we will also begin to identify His *rhema*.

If we are in disobedience and doing something we know God does not approve of, we will lose the connection with God and may not be able to hear Him. The *logos* says that sin separates us from Him. Do not take sin lightly. There is a price to pay when we disobey.

It seems like many people are trying to redefine sin in our modern world. Instead of conforming their lifestyle to the Word of God, some people who know a little about the *logos*, the written Word of God, overuse what I call the "grace card." They say, "Well, God knows my heart, and He forgives me." And yes, that is the problem, God knows the heart. But people sometimes abuse grace as a ticket for compromise. God's grace is not a license to sin but an act of God to show us how much He loves us. Yes, we will sin, but to practice sin or to not be concerned about turning from sin is a very dangerous place to put ourselves. God does not approve of it. Grace provides a great opportunity for us to get right with God, not later but right now.

We do not need to hide from God; He knows what we are doing all the time. It does not matter where we are, He sees us. In the letters to the different churches, Jesus mentions examples such as, "I know your works and I know all the things you do." He is making it very clear He knows what we are doing and that God is all-knowing.

QUESTION

Why does God have a strong desire for us to read, hear and understand what He says?

As He closes these letters to the churches, God emphasizes that He wants us to listen up and hear what He has to say to us. God has such a strong desire for us to read, hear and understand what He has to say to us.

One good way to hear the *rhema* word of God is through reading the *logos*. Before you read the Bible, ask God to speak to you in the passages that you are about to read. Remember that it is important to tune in, and clean out the distractions in your mind. Then take time to meditate on what you just read. Take time to listen; God will reveal things to you in your heart. Then take time to recognize that still, small voice inside.

The hidden manna that Jesus mentions here refers to the time when the children of Israel were wandering in the wilderness. God provided for them by delivering bread from heaven called manna. The Israelites wondered, "What is this?" While the Israelites were wandering in the desert, God gave them the physical blessing of manna to feed them.

In John 6:51, Jesus said, "I am the living bread which came down from heaven. If anyone eats of this bread, he will live forever." Hidden manna represents Jesus Christ, the Bread of Life, who came down from heaven. Everything that Jesus represents is a spiritual blessing. Both uses of manna, physical and spiritual, apply to the children of God. He has declared us righteous and not guilty through faith in Jesus Christ. We feast with Christ today (Revelation 3:20) and will feast with Him in glory.

In verse 17, Jesus says, "And I will give him a white stone, and on the stone a new name written which no one knows except him who receives it." In ancient times, a white stone was used by a judge to vote "not guilty" for a person on trial. White stones have also been given to winners in an athletic contest. So if a person listens and turns away from his sinful desires, he will not only receive the Bread of Life, but will receive the white stone declaring that he is righteous through faith in Jesus Christ.

Just because something may sound good, it does not mean it is. Sometimes, false religions have some good elements mixed in with them. These religions may give to the poor, do humanitarian projects, teach people to be nice to others... the list goes on and on. But no matter how good these organizations may appear on the outside, we must check them for the truth. Jesus must be the center of the church. The Bible must be preached in its entirety. Lastly, this religion must believe that a born-again relationship with Jesus Christ is the only way to receive eternal salvation. If this organization is not aligning with the truth, it is important that you do because your eternal destination depends on it.

Jesus must be the center of the church. The Bible must be preached in its entirety.

The people of Pergamos may have started on the right track, but somewhere they were distracted and went off course. The Lord loved the people in this church so much that He brought correction. This is the same for our lives. The Lord loves each of us so much that He not only brings us correction, but also provides a way to get into right relationship with Him. Thank you, Lord!

What Church Do You Belong To?

CHAPTER FOUR

Thyatira

"And to the angel of the church in Thyatira write: These things says the Son of God, who has eyes like a flame of fire, and His feet like fine brass: I know your works, love, service, faith, and your patience; and as for your works, the last are more than the first. Nevertheless I have a few things against you, because you allow that woman Jezebel, who calls herself a prophetess, to teach and seduce My servants to commit sexual immorality and eat things sacrificed to idols. And I gave her time to repent of her sexual immorality, and she did not repent. Indeed I will cast her into a sickbed, and those who commit adultery with her into great tribulation, unless they repent of their deeds.

I will kill her children with death, and all the churches shall know that I am He who searches the minds and hearts. And I will give to each one of you according to your works. Now to you I say, and to the rest in Thyatira, as many as do not have this doctrine, who have not known the depths of Satan, as they say, I will put on you no other burden. But hold fast what you have till I come. And he who overcomes, and keeps My works until the end, to him I will give power over the nations—. 'He shall rule them with a rod of iron; They shall be dashed to pieces like the potter's vessels'— as I also have received from My Father; and I will give him the morning star. He who has an ear,

let him hear what the Spirit says to the churches" Revelation 2:18-29.

Attributes of Christian Lifestyle

Works
Love
Service
Faith
Patience

Jesus' letter to the church of Thyatira is one that is sent with a strict warning. There are major problems in this church. Often, churches receive problems from the outside that are brought in, but in this church, the problem began on the inside. Take note: Jesus again begins His letter to the church by making it very clear that He is the author.

"And to the angel of the church in Thyatira write, 'These things says the Son of God, who has eyes like a flame of fire, and His feet like fine brass'" (Revelation 2:18).

We might sense that Jesus is upset with this church by the way He describes Himself in verse 18, "who has eyes like a flame of fire." Jesus makes it clear that He knows and sees everything. This church cannot hide anything from Him, and neither can we. Our outward appearance does not necessarily show what is on the inside. Then Jesus said, "His feet are like fine brass." Throughout Scripture, the material of brass represents judgment. So Jesus introduces

Himself as the one who sees all that is happening inside of this church, and who will judge accordingly.

In verse 19, He mentioned five attributes of a Christian lifestyle: works, love, service, faith and patience. These could be considered essentials for a Christian lifestyle. Christians should exemplify these qualities because the Lord is the author of them. People who are not living in Christ have a more difficult time living out these values.

"Nevertheless I have a few things against you, because you allow that woman Jezebel, who calls herself a prophetess, to teach and seduce My servants to commit sexual immorality and eat things sacrificed to idols" (Revelation 2:20).

The leadership or pastor of this church allowed this self-proclaimed prophetess to teach and mislead the church. This false prophetess was leading believers in the wrong direction. This church was engaging in sexual immorality and dabbling in idolatry. Instead of rebuking the false teachings of Jezebel and telling her to hit the road and get out of their church, the leaders in Thyatira allowed her to continue in her deceptive teaching.

Each and every one of us are responsible for our own spirituality. In Matthew 7:15, Jesus gives a warning that we can apply to our lives today. "Beware of false prophets, who come to you in sheep's clothing, but inwardly they are ravenous wolves." We must be on guard to know who is teaching or directing us spiritually.

Now in the letter to the church of Thyatira, Jesus uses the name Jezebel to describe the woman that they allowed into the church to teach. Was Jezebel her real name? It is possible, but not likely. The Old Testament refers to Jezebel as an idolatrous woman who opposed God's ways.

Have you ever met anyone named Jezebel? Most likely you have not. In 1 Kings 21:25, Jezebel was the wife of King Ahab, who led Israel to worship Baal and the sun. Jezebel is described throughout the scriptures in 1st and 2nd Kings. 1 Kings 21:25 "But there was no one like Ahab who sold himself to do wickedness in the sight of the Lord, because Jezebel his wife stirred him up." In 2 Kings 9:22, she is known for her harlotries and witchcraft. Jezebel massacred the prophets of the Lord and was known as a cursed woman. In 2 Kings 9, the story of Jezebel's death is recorded. She was thrown out of a window. Her blood splattered on the walls, horses trampled over her body, and lastly dogs ate her. After all of this, the only thing that was left was her skull, feet and the palms of her hands. The leftover parts of her were then taken and thrown onto a dump site. All of this could be why we do not meet many people are named Jezebel.

QUESTION

How can our sin impact those around us?

Jesus gives a strong description of the Jezebel woman that this church allowed in their "pulpit" to push her own agenda. In Revelation 2:20, Jesus notes that the plan of Jezebel is "to teach and seduce My servants."

48

The word seduce means, "to lead astray, deceive, and cause wandering." This self-proclaimed prophetess Jezebel had a plan, and when she was approved by the church, she convinced the people that the Lord approved of sexual perversion and pagan practices.

> If we allow the wrong people to teach and preach in our churches, the devil will use this as a tool to distract believers from the truth.

There is no doubt that some of Jezebel's teachings had elements of truth, but most of her teachings were false and misled the people away from the Lord. In this very day and age, we can see that false teachings like these have crept their way into some churches. The deceiver, Satan, has a plan to slither his way into our churches and cause us to walk away and abandon the Lord's truth.

What took place in the church in Thyatira was accepted by the people—but in the eyes of Christ it was condemned. The teachings of Jezebel are still condemned by Christ today for our churches and in our own lives.

"And I gave her time to repent of her sexual immorality, and she did not repent" (Revelation 2:21).

To repent means to change your mind. Repentance means accepting God's will for our lives over our own will. It is God's will that none should perish. He does not want us to be separated from Him. However, the plan of the devil is to distract us from the Lord. If we allow the wrong people to teach and preach in our churches, the devil will use this as a tool to distract believers from the truth.

We have a limited time to repent and turn away from evil. Jesus gave Jezebel a limited time to repent. There is an appointed time for each and every one of us to die. We do not know when that time is, which is why we need to get right with the Lord now. In the next couple of verses Jesus lists the consequence of not repenting.

"Indeed I will cast her into a sickbed, and those who commit adultery with her into great tribulation, unless they repent of their deeds" (Revelation 2:22).

It is clear here that each and every one of us is account-able and responsible for the teachings that we follow and believe. We have to make sure that we are doing it right. The foundation for Christian belief is spending time with the Lord in prayer and reading and studying the Bible. Nothing comes before it; nothing replaces it.

God doesn't mess with sin. Sin not only affects us, but also affects those around us. The Lord uses strong words about dealing with sinners. Why does He want to do this? He does it in order to stop sin from spreading.

"I will kill her children with death, and all the churches shall know that I am He who searches the minds and hearts. And I will give to each one of you according to your works" (Revelation 2:23).

We are accountable for what we do. We cannot blame others for our sins, because God will judge our lives individually.

"Now to you I say, and to the rest in Thyatira, as many as do not have this doctrine, who have not known the depths of Satan, as they say, I will put on you no other burden" (Revelation 2:24).

At this point, the deceptive teachings of Jezebel have not completely spread. There are some who did not buy into her sinful teachings. Others, however, did not know the depths of Satan's art or his deceit and fell prey to her deceptive teachings. The art of deceit is teaching man that sinful things are okay when God says that they are wicked.

> The Holy Spirit is always with us to guide us in all things. It is critical that we stay tuned into the Holy Spirit because He will help us discern when something is not right.

"But hold fast what you have till I come" (Revelation 2:25).

The Lord had no special demands for these people who were mislead by the false teaching. He simply wanted them to hold fast to their godly beliefs and resist the evil one. James 4:7 sums this idea up for us and says, "Therefore submit to God. Resist the devil and he will flee from you."

We experience the blessings promised to us when we keep our godly focus as was mentioned in James 4:7. The

Holy Spirit is always with us to guide us in all things. It is critical that we stay tuned into the Holy Spirit because He will help us discern when something is not right. Tuning our ears to hear the Holy Spirit will protect us from wavering and getting distracted and allow us to continue to receive blessings from God.

Good works do not erase the teaching of wrong doctrine. Wrong doctrine may come in the form of compromising biblical truths. Sometimes we may compromise and act on things that are unbiblical because we want to satisfy our flesh. We can never compromise God's word so as to suit our own desires. As a church we can never compromise the Word of God to please others. Sin will always be sin, and no man can change that. The prophetess Jezebel, in the book of Revelation, knew what she was doing was wrong. Even so, she did not repent and turn from her ways. As a result, she received judgment.

QUESTION

How can we guard our hearts and lives from being distracted from God?

God always gives us a way out of sin, but we have to be the one to choose it. If we do not choose to repent and turn from our evil ways, then judgment will definitely come.

It is important that we do not live like the church in Thyatira by tolerating evil or sin in our lives. This grieves the Holy Spirit, and brings judgment. Ask yourself if there is anything coming between you and the Lord. God needs to be first and if He is not first in our lives, over time we will go off course. It may start as being just a couple of degrees off, but over time that sin separates us from the Lord. Many things like tradition, our jobs, hobbies, health, other people and our thoughts can distract us and get in the way of our relationship with God. Again, we need to make sure that God is first in our lives.

The church cannot go along with what the world says. Sometimes this means not being politically correct. Trying to go with what the world says can deviate us from the truth that is found in the Lord. We may not want to hurt someone's feelings, so we will choose to offend God instead. We must always let the truth be told in love.

Christ's message to the Christians in Thyatira is a warning to let them know that they are in serious spiritual danger. The underlying problem is that this church tolerated sin. In a Christian lifestyle, there is no room for sin because sin breeds more sin. Even though there were some good things happening in this church, they were still going off track and heading towards God's judgment.

This is the condition that many people find themselves in even today. In their minds, the good in their life outweighs the bad, and they believe that they are receiving the approval of the Lord. But this is a form of deception from Satan himself. We can be doing good things but be deceived at the same time. There is a lot to be said and understood about this church, but the major point is that God has so much grace and patience for people because of

His love. Because of His love for us, He wrote this letter to the church of Thyatira. We as the church and God's people today can learn from His message.

CHAPTER FIVE

Sardis

"Write this letter to the angel of the church in Sardis: This is the message from the one who has the sevenfold Spirit of God and the seven stars: I know all the things you do, and that you have a reputation for being alive—but you are dead. Wake up! Strengthen what little remains, for even what is left is almost dead. I find that your actions do not meet the requirements of my God. Go back to what you heard and believed at first; hold to it firmly. Repent and turn to me again. If you don't wake up, I will come to you suddenly, as unexpected as a thief. Yet there are some in the church in Sardis who have not soiled their clothes with evil. They will walk with me in white, for they are worthy. All who are victorious will be clothed in white. I will never erase their names from the Book of Life, but I will announce before my Father and his angels that they are mine. Anyone with ears to hear must listen to the Spirit and understand what he is saying to the churches" Revelation 3:1-6 (NLT).

No one likes it when their alarm clock goes off in the morning. We always want just a few more minutes to stay in bed. We will hit the snooze button over and over, until it is the last possible minute that we can get up and still make it to where we need to be on time. The alarm noise interrupts our comfort. Some people do a similar thing in the spiritual realm. They continue to hit their spiritual snooze button and say, "I am comfortable where I am, I am not bothering anyone and no one is bothering me." Living a life that is spiritually asleep is like living a life that is spiritually dead. Jesus is telling the church of Sardis to wake up and be alert.

This church appears to have it all together spiritually, just like many people today give off the appearance of having a relationship with the Lord. Some people come to church on Sunday and act like a Christian, but do not live a godly life the rest of the week. They fool people, their pastor and even themselves, but the Lord knows the truth. It is time to stop trying to fool everyone and wake up.

> Living a life that is spiritually asleep is like living a life that is spiritually dead.

In this letter, Jesus sends a strong message to the church of Sardis that can be applied to our lives today. The church in Sardis was not like the other churches, they were not deep in sin and they were not experiencing any great trials or persecution. As a matter of fact, they appeared as if they were doing fine. Even so, Jesus sees that there is something missing in this church. He warns them to stop going through the motions and losing their passion for God, and if they do not do something about it, they are going to hit a flatline spiritually.

Jesus once again begins this letter identifying Himself as its author: "Write this letter to the angel of the church in Sardis. This is the message from the one who has the sevenfold Spirit of God and the seven stars: 'I know all the things you do, and that you have a reputation for being alive—but you are dead'" (Revelation 3:1-6, NLT).

In this passage, Jesus gives His credentials. When He mentions "the one who has the sevenfold Spirit of God and the seven stars," He is referring to the seven attributes to the Holy Spirit mentioned in Isaiah 11:2: "The Spirit of the Lord shall rest upon Him, The Spirit of wisdom and understanding, The Spirit of counsel and might, The Spirit of knowledge and the fear of the LORD." The sevenfold Spirit is the Holy Spirit. Biblically, the number seven is the number that symbolizes perfection. In Isaiah, we see that when God's Spirit is upon Jesus, then there is wisdom, understanding, counsel, strength, knowledge and fear of the Lord, meaning reverence.

"I know all the things you do, you have a reputation for being alive—but you are dead" (Revelation 3:1, NLT).

Jesus makes a point to the church. He tells them that they are spiritually empty, and even though they may see some appearances of God in their lives, they are about to die.

We can fool a lot of people when we seem to be or appear to be alive. We can look well-polished and groomed on the outside, but God is the one doing the MRI on our hearts. He can speak to our hearts because He can see what is actually going on inside of it. Some may think their great upbringing in the Lord or their past godly works make them alive in Christ. But it is important to recognize that the things in our past do not count for our present condition. This church appeared to be full of faithful believers, but in actuality, they were not following Him properly. People can be spiritually dead because they follow God on their own terms. God's view is different and His view is what counts.

> When our Bibles have been closed, we cannot say that we cannot hear from God. It is important to stay awake in the Word of the Lord.

"Wake up! Strengthen what little remains, for even what is left is almost dead. I find that your actions do not meet the requirements of my God" (Revelation 3:2).

Jesus gives the church of Sardis a warning. He tells them that they are on life support. At times in our life, we may be sleep-walking through life. Now is the time to get up from sleep-walking through life and make some repairs. If your relationship with God is fading and you are in a state of spiritual slumber, it will lead to sin and death. Jesus gives the church of Sardis a sense of hope by encouraging them and reminding them that they are not dead yet. There is still time to make some changes and get back into the game and play by God's rules.

Christ had investigated what the Christians of Sardis had done and warned them that their actions were not matching up to God's standards. In verse 3, the Lord gives us three keys to turn this around.

QUESTION

Do you remember when you first came to the Lord?

"Go back to what you heard and believed at first; hold to it firmly. Repent and turn to me again. If you don't wake up, I will come to you suddenly, as unexpected as a thief" (Revelation 3:3).

Jesus says, "Go back!" Do you remember when you first came to the Lord? There was a great excitement! You told people about it, went to church every Sunday, received answers to prayers and read your Bible. Jesus is saying that you should go back to this exciting time in your life!

Many times when we have a problem in life, we ourselves are the ones to blame. If someone who is married is not taking the time to invest in their marriage, over time the relationship will fade. Our relationship with the Lord is like a marriage. We need to keep it fresh and new. If not, complacency can set in. Complacency can cause us to get comfortable, and comfort can cause us to fall asleep.

Then Jesus said, "You heard." When we have heard something, we do not have an excuse when we disobey. We must get back to listening to Him! We will hear from

God when we are awake, when we listen and direct our attention to Him.

When our Bibles have been closed, we cannot say that we cannot hear from God. It is important to stay awake in the Word of the Lord.

"Go back to what you heard and believed at first"(Revelation 3:3).

Do you remember when you were hungry for the Lord? When you spent time with Him, reading your Bible and praying regularly? At times, you felt God's presence right there with you in the situations you were in. You have seen Him at work. God has not walked away from you, but you have walked away from Him. We need to get back to the place where we first believed. Do not allow yourself to slip away from God. This is the time to "hold to it firmly." Stay on guard, and keep your personal radar on so you do not slip away again.

> If we are truly listening to God, He will speak to us.

"Go back to what you heard and believed at first; hold to it firmly. Repent and turn to me again. If you don't wake up, I will come to you suddenly, as unexpected as a thief"(Revelation 3:3).

Again, we see the word "repent." Jesus is speaking to the Christians in the church at Sardis. We need to make sure that we are ready for our encounter with the Lord.

"Yet there are some in the church in Sardis who have not soiled their clothes with evil. They will walk with me in white, for they are worthy" (Revelation 3:4).

There were some in this dead, sleeping church who loved the Lord. The Lord Himself knew which people were awake. Even today, this is the case in a lot of churches. Some people are sleeping, and some are awake. Some are dead, and others are alive. Pastors need to encourage and wake up their churches.

Next, in verse 5, the Lord shares His promise with those who are awake:

"All who are victorious will be clothed in white. I will never erase their names from the Book of Life, but I will announce before my Father and his angels that they are mine" (Revelation 3:5).

Take note of what Jesus does for us; He gives us a referral to God. He tells the Father, "This guy was sleeping, but now he is awake." It is amazing that no matter what, God is always on our side.

And Jesus closes with this instruction for us:

"Anyone with ears to hear must listen to the Spirit and understand what he is saying to the churches" (Revelation 3:6).

If we are truly listening to God, He will speak to us. The church of Sardis did not receive any compliment from the Lord on their report card, only constructive criticism.

If the Lord looked at your life, what would you receive on your report card? Would He say you are working with all of your heart or that you became complacent and comfortable? Maybe over time your hunger and excitement for the Lord has faded. But as we see in this letter, even if that is the case, our situation is not hopeless in the eyes of the Lord. So, I challenge you to look at your life. Are you alive in Christ or asleep? Maybe God is trying to wake you up!

> We need to actively pursue Him, striving at all times to draw closer to Him.

Complacency is a dangerous place to be. Unfortunately, being complacent in our relationship with the Lord is common. This is when we become too comfortable and are not pursuing our relationship with the Lord. Complacency happens in marriages all the time. The marriage starts out strong; it is fun and exciting. As time passes, the fun slowly slips away; the excitement disappears. Through this process, the communication also slows down to almost zero, and the couple only talks about what is essential. This is a miserable place to be in any relationship, but reaching that place is usually a gradual process.

Marriages do not start out this way, but it is very easy for the relationship to cool off and go on a downward spiral when there is no intentional effort to keep it strong. So it is with our relationship with God. We need to actively pursue Him, striving at all times to draw closer to Him. It is our own responsibility to pursue our relationship with the Lord, not the responsibility of a pastor or a spiritual leader. Though God will give us people to help us along the way, it is still up to us as individuals to make sure we are not getting complacent in our relationship with the Lord.

We might see the evidence of spiritual complacence in different ways. Sometimes, a person's commitment to the local church begins to wear off because they have other things to do on Sunday. The excuses are endless, but this is just one sign of being complacent—and it is dangerous. The person may begin to slow down in their prayer life and Bible reading. As they slow down, it will actually come to a stop. Often, this person still thinks he or she is "okay" spiritually. We must beware of the complacency in our lives. Shake it up, light the fire, and bring that relationship back to life.

What Church Do You Belong To?

CHAPTER SIX

Philadelphia

"And to the angel of the church in Philadelphia write: These things says He who is holy, He who is true, He who has the key of David, He who opens and no one shuts, and shuts and no one opens: I know your works. See, I have set before you an open door, and no one can shut it; for you have a little strength, have kept My word, and have not denied My name. Indeed I will make those of the synagogue of Satan, who say they are Jews and are not, but lie—indeed I will make them come and worship before your feet, and to know that I have loved you. Because you have kept My command to persevere, I also will keep you from the hour of trial which shall come upon the whole world, to test those who dwell on the earth. Behold, I am coming quickly! Hold fast what you have, that no one may take your crown. He who overcomes, I will make him a pillar in the temple of My God, and he shall go out no more. I will write on him the name of My God and the name of the city of My God, the New Jerusalem, which comes down out of heaven from My God. And I will write on him My new name. He who has an ear, let him hear what the Spirit says to the churches." Revelation 3:7-13

There is nothing like receiving an encouraging word. Proverbs 16:24 says, "Pleasant words are like a honeycomb, sweetness to the soul and health to the bones." Words can be constructive or destructive. We need to choose what we say wisely. There is a saying about using words that warns us: "When in doubt, don't let them out."

After reading through the first few letters to the churches, we begin to wonder whether there is any church existing during this time that has people who are actually following the Lord. Next we come to the church in Philadelphia that receives an encouraging letter from the Lord. It shows us that this particular church body is one of faithful.

"And to the angel of the church in Philadelphia write, These things says He who is holy, He who is true, He who has the key of David, He who opens and no one shuts, and shuts and no one opens" (Revelation 3: 7).

As always, Jesus makes it very clear that He is the author of this letter. He addresses this letter to the church in Philadelphia, which by definition means "brotherly love." Brotherly love is a main ingredient for churches. Love needs to be a permanent part of a Christian's life as well as the life of the church. Jesus also identifies Himself by some of His attributes, saying "He is Holy." God's essential characteristic is holiness, the total absence of sin. Jesus makes a clear claim here that He has no sin. He is a Deity; He is God.

Some believe that Jesus was just a great teacher. If Jesus were just a Rabbi or a teacher, He would have gotten upset with Thomas when, in John 20:28, Thomas addressed Jesus as "My Lord and my God." We must always use the Lord's name properly and not take His name in vain. God even warns us in Deuteronomy 5:11, "You shall not take the name of the Lord your God in vain, for the Lord will not hold him guiltless who takes His name in vain." Vain, means "empty" or "false." It is so sad when we hear people use God's name in vain, and even worse when a person who is supposed to have a relationship with the Lord uses God's name in vain. God is not going to let us off the hook for the words we speak.

"These things says He who is holy, He who is true" (Revelation 3:7).

Throughout Scripture, Jesus identifies who He is. There are many belief systems

> Jesus said to him, "I am the way, the truth, and the life. No one comes to the Father except through Me"" John 14:6

that teach different ways to get to heaven, such as being a good person, doing the right thing, or helping others. The list could go on. These are not bad things but they will not get you to heaven. Jesus makes it very clear in John 14:6 that there is only one way to reach God, "I am the way, the truth, and the life. No one comes to the Father except through Me." Note, He says He is the way, the truth and the life. He does not say that He is "a" way or "a" truth. There are not many roads that lead to God or lead to heaven, Jesus is the only way. We must make sure that we are not on the wrong path because it will lead us to the wrong destination. The destination that we are moving toward is the destination for eternity.

"He who has the key of David, He who opens and no one shuts, and shuts and no one opens" (Revelation 3:7).

In this scripture, Jesus reminds us of His power. In Isaiah 22:22, figuratively speaking, King David held the key or authority to Israel. This included all his royal household, military buildings, and even the government. Typically, the person who has the keys to something is the one who is in charge. The person with the keys is the person who will decide for whom to open (or not open) the door. There is a reason for having a lock on a door; it is because not everyone is allowed to enter. The only people who are allowed into a household or other buildings are those who are approved by the owner. Notice that there is only one key, not many keys that will open a door. Jesus is the key and the only way to the Father. There are many people that believe in God or a god, but there is only One True God, and Jesus is the only way we connect with Him. Remember, God the Father, God the Son and God the Holy Spirit are the divine Three-in-One.

After the brief introduction to this church in Philadelphia, Jesus turns things around in verse 8 when speaking to this church. He says, "I know your works..." (Revelation 3:8). It is important to remember that God knows what is happening in our lives. Yes, this means He knows everything about us, our good and bad sides. He knows when we participate in sin, and He knows when we are good to others. He also knows our pain and suffering. However, in one sense, He is keeping score. In Hebrews 6:10 (NLT), it says, "For God is not unjust. He will not forget how hard you have worked for Him and how you have shown your love to Him by caring for other believers, as you still do." God does want each one of us to be a doer of the Word not just a hearer. We were put on the planet by God to do His work, which is spreading the gospel. Our lives need to reflect holiness because He is watching us and so are others.

"See, I have set before you an open door, and no one can shut it" (Revelation 3:8).

One of the ways to know the will of God is by recognizing the doors that are opening and closing in your life. The key is that He is the guide and we must follow Him. Where He guides, He will provide. Often times, we want to go our own way. We walk away from God's will and then ask Him to bless what we are doing. Throughout Scripture, we are exhorted to tune into the Lord. Life is full of distractions and static that will try to distract us. Each of us needs to make a continuous effort to stay in tune with the Lord. As we stay tuned in to Him, we will begin to discern the closed doors from the open ones.

If we take a minute to review our past and evaluate moments in our lives, we can see where God has opened and closed doors. Often times, we want God to move immediately. If God does not, we will bang down the door. Sometimes we get tired of waiting, and we force situations and push doors open. As we trust in God, we will accept the doors that He closes in order to find the ones that are open. We must learn how to accept His "no" in order to receive His "yes." As we learn how to wait and trust in the Lord, He will open the right doors in our lives. Proverbs 16:3 (NLT) says, "Commit your actions to the Lord, and your plans will succeed."

QUESTION

How can we recognize what doors are from the Lord and which ones are from the enemy?

At all times, we are in a battle against the evil one. The devil may show us many pretty, shiny doors, but we must recognize which doors are from the Lord. As we commit each situation in our lives to the Lord, He will direct us. So I want to encourage you to tune into God so that your plans and His plans will fall into place.

Jesus notes something about the church of Philadelphia. He says, "for you have a little strength." Without the Lord in our lives, we are very weak. However, God gives Paul a great word that we can apply to our lives today. Philippians 4:13 says, "I can do all things through Christ who strengthens me." Walking in the will of God will bring us strength. Even through their weakest times, the church of Philadelphia stayed tuned into God.

"They have kept My word, and have not denied My name" (Revelation 3:8).

This word kept means "to keep, to guard, and to watch over." Jesus is saying that this church has not changed the Word of God in order to accommodate their own belief. They have not watered it down, compromised it or ignored it. They have kept the true Word intact and have protected it. It is dangerous to compromise the Word of God so that we will feel better about ourselves. The Bible should always be challenging and changing us. As we study the Word of God, it will help us stay connected to truth.

When we are not reading the Word of God, it is easier to become deceived. Knowing the truth will help us recognize deception. Jesus warns us in Matthew 24:4, "Take heed that no one deceives you." He is telling us something very important: it takes effort to stay true to the Lord. If we do not make that effort, deception will sneak in. When we are not reading our Bibles, it is easier for deception to influence us. Many people think they have a relationship with the Lord, but they are only deceiving themselves. We should want to be like the church of Philadelphia in the fact that they kept His word and did not deny it. If Jesus looked at our lives today, would He find this trait?

"Indeed I will make those of the synagogue of Satan, who say they are Jews and are not, but lie—indeed I will make them come and worship before your feet, and to know that I have loved you" (Revelation 3:9).

One of the marks of Satan's activities is deception. He works to make counterfeit versions of the things of God. And Paul explains in 2 Corinthians 11:13-14, "For such are false apostles, deceitful workers, transforming themselves into apostles of Christ. And no wonder! For Satan himself transforms himself into an angel of light." Regardless of their claims of being Jewish, the people mentioned in Revelation 3:9 are not living a godly lifestyle. They had rejected God's Son. Christ said it plainly: they were of their father, the devil. Jesus is saying that unbelievers amongst them should be able to identify a difference in a believer's lifestyle. They will see that God is on the side of a believer, and unbelievers will want what a believer has in the Lord. This church was a great influence on others. We also are destined to influence others for the Lord. Unbelievers should be able to see something different and attractive in our lives.

"Because you have kept My command to persevere, I also will keep you from the hour of trial which shall come upon the whole world, to test those who dwell on the earth" (Revelation 3:10).

When we are obedient to the Lord, He promises to protect us. This promise from the Lord starts with the word "because." He says "because" you have stayed faithful to the Lord, "because" you held the course, "because" you persevered and did not give up or give in, He is making this promise. God will keep those out of the trouble that is coming to the world, which are said to be a trial for the unsaved and a trial to bring sinners to repentance. What a great promise the Lord gave to this church in Philadelphia that can be applied to our lives today.

"Behold, I am coming quickly! Hold fast what you have, that no one may take your crown" (Revelation 3:11).

We should be able to recognize characteristics of a true Christian's lifestyle: staying the course, living a holy life, having faith, persevering and tuning in to God. Again, we all need to work on maintaining these values. This warning reminds us to continually live a godly lifestyle and trust in Him because we do not know when He is coming again. We need to hold fast to Him in our faith and service.

> When we are obedient to the Lord, He promises to protect us.

"He who overcomes, I will make him a pillar in the temple of My God, and he shall go out no more. I will write on him the name of My God and the name of the city of My God, the New Jerusalem, which comes down out of heaven from My God. And I will write on him My new name" (Revelation 3:12).

When Jesus addresses "He who overcomes," He is talking about the believer, and the reward He mentions is a place in heaven. God is claiming you for heaven.

"He who has an ear, let him hear what the Spirit says to the churches" (Revelation 3:13).

It is important for each of us to take time to stop, look, listen and hear what the Spirit is speaking to our hearts. We have no excuse for not hearing His voice. God is speaking, and we need to tune in, grow and obey. The church in Philadelphia passed the test. It is a church that we should learn from and pattern our lives and churches after. So I encourage you, guard the Word within you, obey the Word in you, be loyal to the Word in you and stay tuned in to God.

CHAPTER SEVEN

Laodicea

"And to the angel of the church of the Laodiceans write, 'These things says the Amen, the Faithful and True Witness, the Beginning of the creation of God: I know your works, that you are neither cold nor hot. I could wish you were cold or hot. So then, because you are lukewarm, and neither cold nor hot, I will vomit you out of My mouth. Because you say, 'I am rich, have become wealthy, and have need of nothing'—and do not know that you are wretched, miserable, poor, blind, and naked—I counsel you to buy from Me gold refined in the fire, that you may be rich; and white garments, that you may be clothed, that the shame of your nakedness may not be revealed; and anoint your eyes with eye salve, that you may see. As many as I love, I rebuke and chasten. Therefore be zealous and repent. Behold, I stand at the door and knock. If anyone hears My voice and opens the door, I will come in to him and dine with him, and he with Me. To him who overcomes I will grant to sit with Me on My throne, as I also overcame and sat down with My Father on His throne. He who has an ear, let him hear what the Spirit says to the churches" (Revelation 3:14-22).

On a hot day, the last thing we want is a warm cup of water. You may even be really thirsty, but a cup of warm water is still disgusting. Even though it is water, the temperature makes all the difference. Do you ever notice how people like iced coffee or hot coffee? No one ever places an order for lukewarm coffee.

Jesus now addresses the church in Laodicea. This church was what He had called a lukewarm church. We will see here that the lukewarm church is in critical condition. This church receives a verbal lashing from Jesus because it has become complacent. Out of all of the seven churches that we have examined, this church could be the closest to resembling the modern day church.

"And to the angel of the church of the Laodiceans write: These things says the Amen, the Faithful and True Witness, the Beginning of the creation of God" (Revelation 3:14).

As always, Jesus starts His letter with His biography. Jesus makes it very clear that this letter is written to the church in Laodicea. He wants to assure the church where His authority comes from. It is interesting as we see the word "Amen." Often times, prayers are ended with the word "Amen," which means "so let it be." It is a way of putting a seal on something. Also, the word "Amen" in Hebrew means "true." In this scripture, the word "Amen" is used as a proper name. When Jesus says the "Amen" at the beginning, it is like He is saying He is the Faithful and True Witness, the beginning of the creation. He is making it very clear that He has the first and final word as well as everything in between. It is confirmed by Scripture that Jesus is the Alpha and the Omega. He is the first and the last, the beginning and the end. Jesus is clear that He is saying He is the source of all creation, and not the result of creation.

"I know your works, that you are neither cold nor hot. I could wish you were cold or hot" (Revelation 3:15).

Jesus was doing an illustrated sermon with this church. The church of Laodicea was located in a place where there was no real water supply. This church had to bring water in from miles away. Because of the journey, the water would warm up to a lukewarm temperature. The Lord used this illustration to explain His complaint to the church. This church appeared to hit rock bottom spiritually, but they did not know it. In verse 16, He describes three types of people in the church: hot, cold, and lukewarm.

"So then, because you are lukewarm, and neither cold nor hot, I will vomit you out of My mouth" (Revelation 3:16).

Jesus has the problem with those who, He calls lukewarm, because there is no such thing as being a lukewarm Christian, church or church body. If we are living lukewarm, we are not truly a Christian. A lukewarm person is someone who says they believe in Jesus but does not live as a true believer. The hot ones are those that are truly saved. The cold ones are the group of people who are not believers and do not claim to be believers; they are sinners on their way to hell.

Jesus is telling this church to wake up! A lukewarm church will produce lukewarm members. A lukewarm person might experience some of what God is doing and get an emotional high, but their lifestyle has not been changed. In this church, there has been no real change or true conversions because there was no desire for more of God in the first place. This church was just experiencing an emotion, but feelings and emotions do not genuinely change a person.

> The lukewarm ones are the religious guys, such as the Pharisees.

When we look at different people in the Bible, we can identify them as cold, hot or lukewarm. The cold ones are the harlots, and the hot ones are the apostles and true followers of Christ. The lukewarm ones are the religious guys, such as the Pharisees.

Have you ever been around a person who just makes you sick? This church made Jesus sick. We all like hot soup, not lukewarm soup. Lukewarmness is useless and good for nothing.

"I will vomit you out of My mouth" (Revelation 3:16).

To vomit forth means "to show utter rejection, to projectile vomit, and to reject with extreme disgust." Some of the churches that we have studied have made Jesus angry, but this one made Him so sick that He wanted to vomit.

The difference between those who are hot and those who are cold is the temperature. When Jesus is explaining the temperature of this church, He is talking about the spiritual temperature of its people. When He says cold, He is speaking of a spiritual condition. A cold person is someone who is not saved. A hot person is one who is saved. Those are the only conditions because if you are lukewarm, your spiritual condition is equal to being cold. Jesus says He would rather deal with the hot or cold ones. There is more hope for the cold ones to heat up than the lukewarm ones. A self-righteous person may think by their own theology that they are in the right place with the Lord, but these are the ones that make Jesus vomit. These people are the ones who are spiritually dead.

"Because you say, 'I am rich, have become wealthy, and have need of nothing'—and do not know that you are wretched, miserable, poor, blind, and naked" (Revelation 3:17).

Over thousands of years, many things have not changed. People are in the pursuit of physical things, like money. The church of Laodicea was one of the wealthiest of the seven churches. This church had everything it needed. Jesus reminds them that they are being deceived. They think that they are rich, wealthy, and don't need anything. They have no idea that they are really miserable, poor, blind and naked.

People may think they are happy because they have a lot of money, but in reality their life needs some major work.

This church was afflicted but did not even realize their own condition; they were spiritually blind and did not even know it. Some may think that material possessions can be a sign of spiritual blessings, but that is not always the case. Many wealthy people are godly people, but some are not. Chasing after riches is a dangerous and slippery slope. People will sacrifice their families, relationship with the Lord, health and so much more in the pursuit of money. One of the devil's greatest tricks is to lure people with money. Many people believe that they are working hard for their family and for a better future, meanwhile their marriage, family and very self are deteriorating around them. Jesus is warning this church, and us, not to be deceived. These people were content and did not recognize their need. If we are not careful, the pursuit of riches can lead us astray.

> Like a good father, the Lord brings correction to His children so as to help them return to the right path.

The unhealthy desire for money, also known as greed, affects our relationship with the Lord. Jesus uses an illustration in Matthew 19:24 (KJV) to demonstrate this concept. He said, "It is easier for a camel to go through the eye of a needle, than for a rich man to enter into the kingdom of God." Jesus is not saying that it is impossible for a rich man to enter the kingdom of God, but He is sending a warning message that the unhealthy desire for money will be a distraction. Our number one desire in life should be for the Lord.

This church of Laodicea was a light but also allowed darkness to come in.

"I counsel you to buy from Me gold refined in the fire, that you may be rich; and white garments, that you may be clothed, that the shame of your nakedness may not be revealed; and anoint your eyes with eye salve, that you may see" (Revelation 3:18).

QUESTION

How does the Lord use correction to show His love for us?

Jesus is saying, "Listen to Me!" He wanted them to find the real spiritual treasures and gold that He had to offer. He wanted them to stop looking elsewhere, but to find their riches in Him. Many things in our lives will blind us from seeing the truth. The only way to see the truth is to have a personal relationship with the Lord Jesus through Bible reading and prayer. A personal relationship with the Lord will open our eyes to the truth through His Word.

"As many as I love, I rebuke and chasten. Therefore be zealous and repent" (Revelation 3:19).

Like a good father, the Lord brings correction to His children so as to help them return to the right path. Jesus said that because of His love for them, He could not tolerate the way they were; it was making Him sick. John 3:16 says, "For God so loved the world that He gave His only begotten Son, that whoever believes in Him should not perish but have everlasting life." Our desire for God should cause us to want to repent. God also says in Revelation 3:19 that we need to burn with zeal so we would want to repent. Something needs to burn in our hearts. Repentance is our choice, but also God's desire for us. Repentance is accepting our wrongness and changing our direction by 180 degrees and bringing our will into alignment with the Lord's will for our lives. God makes it very clear that without repentance there is no forgiveness of sin and no relationship with Lord. Repentance means that we realize that we are guilty, we are sinners, and we are heading to hell. Repentance means that we turn away from all sin. Our sin cannot be remedied on our own.

"Behold, I stand at the door and knock. If anyone hears My voice and opens the door, I will come in to him and dine with him, and he with Me" (Revelation 3:20).

It is amazing that God desires for us to be in relationship with Him. He literally came down to the earth to seek us out. As a matter a fact, He came to us while we were still sinners. Even while we were His enemy, He still came looking for us.

Isn't it interesting that God has an unending love for us? He does not give up on us. The word stand in this verse means "stood, stand, and continue to stand." Similarly, the word knock in this verse means "knock, knocked, knocking, and knocks." The words are used in the past, present and future tense. Jesus will not give up on us because of His relentless love for us. Even though Jesus was not happy with the people in the church of Laodicea, He was still standing and knocking on their door because He wanted to have a relationship with them. Just like Jesus wanted to be on the inside of this church, He wants to be on the inside of our hearts and have our full attention. He wants to dine with us and share supper, the main meal of the day, with us. Sometimes this meal extends for several hours because of fellowship around the table.

We can recognize from these verses two things about God: He wants to be in relationship with us for all of eternity and He can be accessible for the here and now. God loves us so much that He is concerned about our everyday lives. 1 Peter 5:7 says, "Cast all your cares upon Him, for He cares for you."

"To him who overcomes I will grant to sit with Me on My throne, as I also overcame and sat down with My Father on His throne" (Revelation 3:21).

> Repentance is our choice, but also God's desire for us.

1 John 5:5 (NIV) says, "Who is it that overcomes the world? Only the one who believes that Jesus is the Son of God." The overcomers are those who believe in the Lord. It seems pretty easy—all that needs to be done is to believe. Don't most people believe in Jesus? The question is, what does the word "believe" really mean? Believe means to absolutely, one hundred percent, put our trust in Jesus. When everything is going well, this seems easy. But what happens

when the road gets a little bumpy? Do we go directly to the Lord, or do we try to figure out things on our own? This is a good test to gauge the position of our relationship with Him. Those who overcome do so by trusting in Christ and remaining unwavering in their faith, even when the road gets bumpy.

"He who has an ear, let him hear what the Spirit says to the churches" (Revelation 3:22).

Jesus closes His letter to the church of Laodicea in the same way He has closed all of His letters to the other churches. He exhorts us to hear what the Spirit of God is saying.

Wouldn't it be great if we gave the Lord as much attention as we give our cell phones? We are always looking for a text, checking emails, checking Facebook and engaging with other forms of social media. When we are in relationship with the Lord, we will hear His voice. We need to tune back into Him.

When something cold is heated up, it begins to boil. A recognizable change takes place. We need to ask ourselves, "Does my faith really mean something to me? Has it changed my life?" A lukewarm Christian only seeks God when things in life are difficult. They do not regularly share their faith, they somehow rationalize and take part in sin without any remorse, their prayers do not come from the heart, and they go to church to feel something good rather than to hear from the Lord. Remember, God's desire for us is to be hot, not cold or lukewarm. Ask yourself, are you a lukewarm Christian?

What Church Do You Belong To?

CHAPTER EIGHT

The Purpose of the Church

Have you ever asked yourself, "What is my purpose in life?" It is a very sad place to be in if you are just existing. It is sad when you do not know what you are doing or where you want to go in life—when there is no direction or manual for your life. Maybe your friends are established with a good career and have started a family, and you ask yourself, "What about me?"

Many businesses have a vision and a plan that defines their purpose. This is good, but merely having a plan or a purpose does not guarantee success. Many people would like to own their own business and make a lot of money. Many people have good ideas, but never take the next step because they are afraid they will fail. Having the good intention of finding your purpose, whether in life or in business, is not good enough. It would be like driving across the country without a map. There is no doubt that you really want to get to the other coast, but without a plan to guide you, you will not end up in the right place. If you can follow the plan and stay on the course without giving up, you can achieve what you set out to do.

When you achieve your plan or purpose, you achieve fulfillment. God has a plan and a purpose both for your life and for the church. These two go hand in hand. To fulfill our God-given purpose in life, we need the church and the church needs us. God's purpose for the church is to spread the gospel, so that people will come to the saving knowledge of Jesus Christ.

> God has a plan and a purpose, both for your life and for the church. These two go hand in hand.

It is easy to see the purpose, but how do we get there? It is achieved through the church. We might look at the church as a building or a group of people, but in reality, it is the individuals that make up the church. Each person who has given his or her life over to Jesus is now a member of the church, the one and only church that Jesus designed and built.

In a business, everyone who is employed at the company has a job to do. They are not being paid to stand around all day; they were hired for a reason and are expected to complete a task. Whether the company has ten people employed or ten thousand, each and every person is to do a job that contributes to the success of the company. Work is expected and required from each employee. In a smaller company, there might only be one person doing a specific task, but in a larger company, there may be multiple people doing the same job. Regardless, each person plays an important role in fulfilling the purpose of the company, which is to achieve the finished product. As a member of the church, we also have to do our part in achieving God's plan.

Within the church, every person is important. Every person has a part to play or a obligation to fulfill. Your talents are not really yours, but they are talents given by God to each and every one of us. They are designed and given to you by God for the fulfillment of His mission for your life. Many people have gifts and talents that are not being used for God. It is sad to see a musician who can play an instrument wonderfully or who has a voice that can bring down the house, but does not use it to glorify God. Although every gift comes from God, a person who does not have a personal relationship with the Lord will claim credit for their own gifting. As Christians we must use our talents to serve the plan of the Lord and spread the gospel. We as the church, the people of God, are to operate as one and use our gifts to complete the church in the mission set before us.

Every person has a job to do. A person can do many jobs for the Lord, but typically, one particular job is their strength. For example, not everyone has the primary gifting of a teacher, but in some areas, we still may be able to teach. We cannot limit ourselves and say "I am not an evangelist so I will not try to act like one," because all believers are called to evangelize. We all have strengths and weakness in certain areas, but even in our weaknesses, God is strong.

This brings us to another major point: God is our strength. It is God who can do the work through us. As we grow in the Lord, we can recognize His power in us. We begin to rise up and handle responsibilities as we learn to trust more and more in the Lord. At times we will even surprise ourselves, but this is God working in and through us.

In the following verses, Paul explains God's design for His plan.

"For as the body is one and has many members, but all the members of that one body, being many, are one body, so also is Christ. For by one Spirit we were all baptized into one body—whether Jews or Greeks, whether slaves or free—and have all been made to drink into one Spirit. For in fact the body is not one member but many. If the foot should say, 'Because I am not a hand, I am not of the body,' is it therefore not of the body? And if the ear should say, 'Because I am not an eye, I am not of the body,' is it therefore not of the body? If the whole body were an eye, where would be the hearing? If the whole body were hearing, where would be the smelling? But now God has set the members, each one of them, in the body just as He pleased. And if they were all one member, where would the body be? But now indeed there are many members, yet one body. And the eye cannot say to the hand, 'I have no need of you'; nor again the head to the feet, 'I have no need of you.' No, much rather, those members of the body which seem to be weaker are necessary. And those members of the body which we think to be less honorable, on these we bestow greater honor; and our unpresentable parts have greater modesty, but our presentable parts have no need. But God composed the body, having given greater honor to that part which lacks it, that there should be no schism in the body, but that the members should have the same care for one another. And if one member suffers, all the members suffer with it; or if one member is honored, all the members rejoice with it. Now you are the body of Christ, and members individually" (1 Corinthians 12:12-27).

These verses tells you how important you are for God's plan for the church. We all have shortcomings and weaknesses. In some areas, we are weak, but in others we are stronger. Where one has weakness, another has strength. When the body of Christ is knitted together, we join to make a strong church. This is for the purpose of achieving God's purpose for His design of the church. It is a plan that has worked and is still working, through each and every one of us.

When there is a purpose being worked out, it comes with difficulties. During times of difficulties, we need help from within. At times, the load is too heavy to lift on our own, so we need someone to help with the lifting. Sometimes something breaks apart, and we need someone to help put it back together. At other times, we may get frustrated, so we need someone to encourage us. We need each other.

Many dynamics take place within the church. Many things happen, and should happen, among those who assemble together. Your church is a place to learn about God and the Bible. Let's take a look at the following verses and different components that make up God's plan.

"And they continued steadfastly in the apostles' doctrine and fellowship, in the breaking of bread, and in prayers" (Acts 2:42).

Notice that they were learning about doctrine, and it was new for the people of that time. They did not have the Bible as we now know it. Also notice that unity takes place. We are to fellowship to the point of eating together, which means spending time with those in the church. Also notice that they were praying together. Prayer is a powerful part of the church.

In verse 43 says, "Then fear came upon every soul, and many wonders and signs were done through the apostles." These are signs, wonders, miracles that will take place in a church in which the Lord resides. One miracle is people giving their life to the Lord Jesus. This is a good gauge of the condition of the church.

"Now all who believed were together, and had all things in common" (Acts 2:44).

We see again the point being made about the unity of the church. Unity comes through and by the Lord. The world is separated by so many things: politics, race, age, religions, beliefs, genders, social status, etc. Christ is the one that unites us together.

"And sold their possessions and goods, and divided them among all, as anyone had need" (Acts 2:45). The church provides for her own. When a member of the church is in need of food, finances, shelter, support, prayer, encouragement or much more, the members of that local assembly are to be there for that person and for that need.

> Church growth is a great indication that God is at work in your assembly.

"So continuing daily with one accord in the temple, and breaking bread from house to house, they ate their food with gladness and simplicity of heart" (Acts 2:45).

The church should be meeting consistently together, whether in church or at one another's homes. Just enjoying each other. Again, unity in the Lord resounds.

"Praising God and having favor with all the people. And the Lord added to the church daily those who were being saved" (Acts 2:47).

A key factor for a church is to be worshipping God. Church is not a place for a social event, where it is all fun and pleasure. There is great fun and pleasure without a doubt. Church is a great place to be, but worshipping God needs to be the key activity. When this plan that God created is at work, people will be getting saved, and the church will be a growing church. Church growth is a great indication that God is at work in your assembly.

Six Observations in the Church

There are several requirements that make up the church that God intended. First, the church must have the proper doctrine. Although this sounds pretty obvious, throughout history many churches have taken from or added to the Word of God. This is the major reason that there are so many different churches. Having the wrong doctrine is very dangerous and earns eternal consequences. It is up to each and every individual to make sure they are going to the right church. At the end of our lives here on earth, we will have to give an account for ourselves; we will not be able to blame others. Our eternity with God can be put into jeopardy if we are following the wrong doctrine. God's Word is the truth, and we must know it for ourselves.

Secondly, God desires unity. This can be found in Scripture. The family unit is God's idea, for both the church and at home. Unity in the home is a sign of wholeness, and so is unity in the church. Remember, God unites and the devil divides. So when you see division in the church, buyer beware. However, when we see division, it is up to each and every one of us to examine what is going on. The devil uses many tricks in his attempts to separate the body of Christ, for example, gossiping about others, judging the pastor's decisions, not to mention the changes that happen within the church. Many people do not like change and they do not have a problem vocalizing their dissatisfaction. There are many reasons for division. Division may even cause people to leave the church. Regardless, God does not like division or disunity.

Thirdly, prayer is a must. Prayer connects us with God, the creator of the church. Members of the church need to pray for one another. They need to pray for protection from the enemy. They need to pray that they will not fall into temptation and sin. They must ask for God's will to be done. The church must pray to see souls saved. As individuals, we need to pray for ourselves and for others. We also need to pray for opportunities to share the gospel with others. Prayer is a part of His church. Prayer is critical. Jesus said in Matthew 21:13, "My house shall be called a house of prayer." This is a requirement and a sign of His church. Remember, there is only one church, the church that Jesus founded.

We may know how to pray to God for our needs, but we are also to pray for God's will to be done in our lives. One of His desires is that none should perish or be separated from Him for eternity. God uses us, the church, to spread His Word. We need to be in deep prayer for our loved ones and everyone we come in contact with. We must pray that we will recognize the opportunities that God gives us on a daily basis. Prayer is required of the church.

The forth requirement is to see miracles happening. Miracles are the evidence that God is at work in the assembly or the church. What greater sign that God resides within the church than to experience the supernatural. For example, when the doctors or the medicine offer no hope, when a couple has given up on their marriage, when a financial disaster occurs. . . then God restores the health, marriage or finances. It is very clear that God did it and it was nothing short of a miracle. It is God's working hand in action. Without the evidence of God at work, the church is just an assembly of people. Without this evidence, the church lacks the power of God. One of the greatest miracles that takes place in the church is people coming to accept Jesus as their Lord and Savior.

> One of the greatest miracles that takes place in the church is people coming to accept Jesus as their Lord and Savior.

Fifth is consistency in lifestyle. The church is not supposed to be a once-a-week or once-in-a-while event. Christianity is a lifestyle. The person who belongs to the church will live according to God's requirements. Many people treat the church as if it were an à la carte menu. They take what they want, when they want it. Some may have good intentions, but are not living their lives according to God's commands. There could be millions of reasons why people are not consistent in attending church. But we are told in Scripture not to neglect coming together. The church is a group of people gathering together. We are not lone rangers who think we do not need the church because we have a personal relationship with God. Such a person is disobedient to God's command and will twist the Word of God to fit his or her own ideas and desires. When you become a Christian, you become the church.

Lastly, a requirement of God's church is praise. God is always worthy to be praised, and it is His desire for us to praise Him. We praise Him in song and with musical instruments. In Scripture, we can see that praising God was a noisy exercise—in a good way. When we really realize what God has done for us, we will definitely praise and thank Him and not be shy about it. In one sense, praise is an outward sign of a grateful heart. We see this in Psalm 33 where praise time is a joyful time. Praising God is something believers should want to do.

The Result

When the church is operating in the proper way, and when these six attributes are taking place naturally, the result is church growth. To grow, there needs to be life. The God-given design of the church will produce this life. Many have seen churches that have not grown in decades, those little church buildings along the road that are older than our grandparents. What is up with that? It appears that something is not happening.

Church leaders must have a living relationship with the Lord. If leaders have never invited Christ in to their hearts and lives, how would Christ come into that congregation? It does not even make sense. When a person comes into a relationship with God, God reveals the Scriptures to them. Without that revelation, they will not be able to understand or identify God and His will. If a church leader does not have relationship with Christ, they are just having some sort of occupation without the real meaning of church leadership.

The next important need for the church is to operate according to God's will. In order for this to happen, the leaders must be following Jesus. Leaders, whether they are pastors, elders or any other office, still need to be led. No leader should go without accountability. We all need to have people we respect, listen to and are accountable to, no matter who we are. It is a dangerous place to be in life when you feel like you don't need anyone's guidance. Marriages fail because of a lack of accountability. Employees get fired for not wanting to be accountable to their bosses. Many, including ministers and church leaders, stray into sin because of lack of submission to authority. This is simply labeled as pride. God says that He will resist the proud.

It is unfortunately common for people to make up their own form of accountability with people who are like-minded. They want others to hold them accountable as long as they agree with what they are saying. Rebellion says, "I will do what I want to do. I will do things my own way, regardless of what anyone thinks." At times, these type of people will even twist Scripture to make it agree with them so they can get what they want.

Real Church Leadership

The Bible explains the church leadership program in Ephesians 1:22-23 (NLT).

"God has put all things under the authority of Christ and has made him head over all things for the benefit of the church. And the church is his body; it is made full and complete by Christ, who fills all things everywhere with himself."

This scripture makes it very clear the church is to be led by one person, Jesus Himself. Jesus, without question, is the leader. Every church leader needs to recognize that and live by that. It needs to be reflected in the leader's life and church's agendas. A visitor into the church assembly should recognize that Jesus is the center and He is the one in charge. At times, people can detect a prideful person, but not all the time. Pride can be disguised in many forms. So, if Jesus is the leader, that means that the church leaders are servants. To be a good leader, you must be a good servant.

The Lord calls the church His body. Jesus is the head of the body. 1 Corinthians 12:12 says, "For as the body is one and has many members, but all the members of that one body, being many, are one body, so also is Christ."

This example of a human body is used to explain how every person or part has a job and needs to function as that part of the body. A foot cannot be a hand. And a hand cannot be an arm. No matter what body part, every part is important so that the body can function fully. God has designed us to function with the parts He has put on us. And we will function well. So believers are a part of the church body. Every one of us is very important.

CHAPTER NINE

The Perfect Church

Jesus is perfect, and His design for the church is perfect as well. However, we are imperfect people. Sin has saturated and influenced each and every one of us since birth. Evil is present in the world and affects each of us. Sin affects our thoughts, our attitudes, emotions, dispositions, responses to others and so much more. Even when we are born again, we still have human attributes that we bring into our assembly that we call the church. We have many differences.

When people come together, it is inevitable that our differences will clash in some form or another. A mature person will have a mature response to these situations. Some people say and do things that they have no business saying or doing. That is a sign of immaturity. The immature people in the church are those that also complain. They complain about things such as the operations of the church, the temperature, the style of music . . . just about anything. But the church may not just have the immature; they may have just plain old cranky people. Maybe they have been in the church forever, but still are not filled with the joy of the Lord. Regardless, the point is that the group of people we assemble with are not perfect. And we cannot expect perfection out of an imperfect group of people.

Paul's Observations and Corrections

However, as we have examined the seven churches of Revelation in-depth, we can identify how each of these churches got off path. To sum it up, it is because of what humans have done and allowed in the church. In Paul's letters to some of the churches, he speaks into specific groups and to their issues specifically. Paul brings the correction that is needed. Centuries later, churches are still struggling with many of the same problems that these early churches experienced. In Paul's first letter to the Corinthians, he addresses the division that they were experiencing within the church.

Division is a major concern for all churches even today. Division has brought many different denominations into existence. Disagreement that is dealt with immaturely will almost always bring separation. However, church leadership must be following their Leader, Jesus. Remember, Jesus is ultimately in charge of the church. He is the head. If you find a church that does not have Jesus in charge, it is a good thing to move on and find a church where He is the leader. Even where Jesus is the leader, we still need to grow up in the Lord and not allow personalities to bring division. It is a serious offense when one tries to separate the body of Christ.

Paul then goes on to explain sexual immorality within the church. A church where sin is not condemned will lead to a church that lives with sin. Some people and even denominations seem to be trying to redefine sin. But there is nothing new under the sun. There is no approval for sin whether it is in the church or outside of it. Leadership is held to a higher standard with higher consequences for sin. No one is above obedience to God. Paul states clearly that we must flee from sexual immorality. Run from sin, do not even entertain it and do not allow it in the door of your home, heart or mind.

> Jesus is ultimately in charge of the church. He is the head. If you find a church that does not have Jesus in charge, it is a good thing to move on and find a church where He is the leader.

Paul writes a lot about Christian behavior. He addresses people who have not made Jesus Lord of their lives and live as their own lord. Such persons do not live by the commands of God but live by their own rules. This is a rebellious lifestyle. However, Paul is speaking to Christians, the members of the body of Christ, and members of His church.

Paul also teaches on marriage, godly parenting, children and their behavior, among other topics. God used Paul to convey His message of the commands, guidelines and major points that Christians need to adhere to. He points out the fact of the death and resurrection of Jesus Christ and explains that there is no other way to heaven but through

Jesus. People cannot earn their way into heaven. Paul tells us our way to heaven is only earned by what Jesus did for us. As sinners, we need to ask God for forgiveness and invite Christ into our lives. These are critical pillars of the gospel. All churches need to proclaim this within their church body. This cannot be denied, and if it is, the church assembly is off its proper course.

Paul also warns of idolatry, which can creep into the church. Idolatry is putting anything before the Lord. Even back in Paul's day, statues were brought into assemblies as some type of sacred object. Paul warns not to have these things because they will occupy the wrong position in our hearts.

In order for the church to fulfill her purpose, these main requirements for the church need to be put into operation.

CHAPTER TEN

The Foundation
of the Church

"For no other foundation can anyone lay than that which is laid, which is Jesus Christ" (1 Corinthians 3:11).

Jesus created the church for specific reasons. He is the foundation and the head of the church; He is the rock that the church is built on. The foundation is obviously critical to any structure or belief system. A foundation is designed to carry the weight of the building, which keeps the structure stable. In a belief system or a church group, the foundation is what supports the belief. Many of these systems have a poor foundation, and many foundations will crack or break under load or stress. Obviously, this affects the followers, directly and indirectly. Many belief systems have come and gone over time because they were not built on the foundation of Jesus.

Colossians 1:18 says, "And He is the head of the body, the church, who is the beginning, the firstborn from the dead, that in all things He may have the preeminence."

Jesus is referred to as the head of the church. This means that all authority comes from Him. In businesses, there is a president. This person leads the operations of the business. He or she has all the authority to make decisions and instructs the employees to fulfill their orders. The president points the direction of the company. In a lot of cases, the president is the founder and has the opportunity to lead in whatever direction he or she wants. The president most likely knows the business better than any of his or her employees. It is critical that an employee follows the leader's rules, and if not, there will be consequences.

> Leaders of the church must recognize that the church is built on Jesus and He is the head.

Leaders of the church must recognize that the church is built on Jesus and He is the head. The teaching or theology of an assembly must adhere to these principles in order to be considered the church. There is only one church, and that is the one that Jesus created. Many assemblies like to call themselves churches, but they do not meet the biblical requirements of the church that Jesus created.

For a church to be the church that Jesus created, He has to be the foundation and the head. He is the founder and the ruling authority. In His word, we learn about the relationship that the Lord desires with us. We also learn what we can do, what we cannot do and how we should treat others. We learn more of the heart of God. We learn what it means to be obedient. These are all crucial, not only for our life here on earth, but also for eternity.

What is between the head and the foundation of the church?

First, we must have a relationship with Jesus Christ—not religion, but relationship. Making Him Lord of your life and having no other gods before Him: no person, no saint, no great human being. You can read more on how to have this relationship in the last chapter.

Secondly, you must belong to a church and not neglect attending it. Hebrews 10:25 (KJV) says, "Not forsaking the assembling of ourselves together, as the manner of some is; but exhorting one another: and so much the more, as ye see the day approaching." Some people believe they do not need to belong to a church, but that is disobedience. God even designed the structure within the church to help us not be rebellious.

Thirdly, there are dynamics that happen within the body of the church. We find and offer encouragement, healing, teaching and learning of Scripture, and much more. We come to understand the purpose of the church. Many things happen within the church assembly.

Fourthly, a church must proclaim a call to action. The major purpose for the church is to spread the gospel, the good news of Jesus Christ. Matthew 5:14-16 says, "You are the light of the world. A city that is set on a hill cannot be hidden. Nor do they light a lamp and put it under a basket, but on a lampstand, and it gives light to all who are in the house. Let your light so shine before men, that they may see your good works and glorify your Father in heaven." God uses His people to spread His message through the world.

We also see Jesus' words that are known as the great commission in Matthew 28:18-20 (NLT):

"Jesus came and told his disciples, 'I have been given all authority in heaven and on earth. Therefore, go and make disciples of all the nations, baptizing them in the name of the Father and the Son and the Holy Spirit. Teach these new disciples to obey all the commands I have given you. And be sure of this: I am with you always, even to the end of the age.'"

In both of these scriptures, we find our duty to fulfill the purpose of the church. As Christians, people are to see Christ in us by our action, behaviors and lifestyles. We will all learn these from what God teaches us in His Word and in His church. But take notice, it is not just about us; it is about directing people to God.

In the great commission, we see Jesus' final instruction to the disciples. He says to "go" and make more disciples. People might say that Jesus was speaking to a certain group of people, and He was. He was speaking to His disciples. If you have made Jesus the Lord of your life, you will desire to follow His teachings. The meaning of disciple is a learner, a follower of Jesus Christ and one who learns the doctrines of God's Word and lives out the lifestyle that is required. In Matthew, we learn that we are to live a godly life so that people will see Christ in us and glorify God. Our lives will point people to a relationship with God. Our godly lives will also teach people who are growing in the Lord and rescue them from being stranded without any direction or purpose.

So Many Churches

You may ask, "How can I find the right church?" They all think they are right—but are they, really? Just because a church has a sign out front that says it's a church, is it really a part of the one that Jesus created? How can we tell?

Nowadays we have a greater advantage with the internet. We can visit a church's website and find a lot of key information. Most websites will look pretty and inviting as well. The website is designed to be appealing to the viewer because most churches want more people to come in and join them.

But we must look past the appearance of the site and look into the church's "statement of faith," "what we believe" and their vision. This is the most important place to start.

Here is what to look for in a church. First you want to see Jesus mentioned a lot. The church needs to be centered around Him. So, it will reflect in their site. Here is an example "statement of faith" with some major points.

STATEMENT OF
FUNDAMENTAL TRUTHS

The Bible is our all-sufficient rule for faith and practice.

The Scripture is divinely inspired.

The One True God as a Trinity: Father, Son, Holy Spirit

The Deity of the Lord Jesus Christ

The Fall of Man

The Salvation of Man

All of these points are critical and set the tone for the spiritual condition of the church. There will be other things, but these listed above are the important ones to look for. Again, Jesus needs to be in the forefront. If you cannot find the statement of faith or church beliefs, beware. If Jesus is not mentioned, again beware. If the Bible is not their main book, beware. Many churches use other writings to supersede the Bible. Nothing can take the place of God's Word, the Holy Bible.

Another basic is that the church's beliefs need to line up with the Bible 100 percent. Some churches have redefined sin so that it fits their comfort level. Nothing has changed in God's Word. Sin is sin. People are sinners and are in need of forgiveness. This can only come by accepting Jesus Christ into their lives. The Word of God teaches us about heaven and hell. We need to do what we can do to make sure we end up in the right place for eternity.

These are just a few of the buzz words to look out for when looking for a church. Many churches are streaming their services online. Watching or listening to an old sermon from a church is a great way to get a feel for their spiritual temperature. As mentioned before, the most important thing about a church is that Jesus is the center, and this should come across loud and clear.

So how can we find a right church for us? There are a lot of right churches out there, where Jesus is Lord is magnified and is at the center.

After doing some homework on a few churches, and if they pass the first test, there is a second test. Let's think of it this way: there are many houses out there, but only one is your home. We know that we are at home as soon as we walk in the door. Many churches are the same way. As soon as someone walks in the door they feel at home.

A lot of times when someone is shopping for a home they will visit many houses that are for sale and yet not feel

> We must find a church that feels like home.

that those homes are "right." There is usually one home, however, that "feels like home" as soon as you walk in the door. Churches are similar.

Even though this "right" feeling is important, we should not base a decision about what church to belong to only on emotion. The key for finding the right church can be found in Matthew 7:7-8: "Ask, and it will be given to you; seek, and you will find; knock, and it will be opened to you. For everyone who asks receives, and he who seeks finds, and to him who knocks it will be opened."

We must ask the Lord to show us what church we should belong to.

So if you are really looking for the right church, God says ask Him, and go out and start looking for it. God promises that you will find it.

CHAPTER ELEVEN

The Most Important Thing for You

Just because someone may be a good person, being good is not good enough. Just because one goes to church, going to church is not good enough. We cannot do anything to earn God in us. There is only one way to have God in you and to experience that relationship we have been talking about in this book. The scriptures below explain God's plan for us. He makes it simple, and He desires this relationship with you.

Confirmation that Jesus is the only way:
John 14:6
"Jesus said to him, 'I am the way, the truth, and the life. No one comes to the Father except through Me.'"

Confirmation that being a good person is not good enough:
Isaiah 64:6
"But we are all like an unclean thing,
And all our righteousnesses are like filthy rags;"

Confirmation that we all start out on a sinking ship:
Romans 3:23
"For all have sinned and fall short of the glory of God."

Confirmation that we are disconnected with God:
Isaiah 59:2 (NLT)
"It is your sins that have cut you off from God..."

Confirmation that we need something new in our lives:
John 3:3
"Jesus answered and said to him,
'Most assuredly, I say to you, unless one is born again,
he cannot see the kingdom of God.'"

Confirmation that He loves us:
1 John 1:9

"If we confess our sins, He is faithful
and just to forgive us our sins and to cleanse us
from all unrighteousness."

Confirmation of His desire for us:
Revelation 3:20
"Behold, I stand at the door and knock.
If anyone hears My voice and opens the door, I will come
in to him and dine with him, and he with Me."

**Confirmation that you want God as your Father
and want to be a part of His church:**
Romans 10:10
"For with the heart one believes unto righteousness, and
with the mouth confession is made unto salvation."

Your eternal destination is determined by the decision you make while here on earth. We are all sinners separated from God. Jesus is the only connection available to us. So we recognize that we are sinners and in need of forgiveness. We have to recognize it and know it. Sin separates us from God. However, if we ask Him for forgiveness, He promises to forgive us.

Jesus said He is knocking at the door of our heart waiting for us to answer. He promises when you invite Him in, He will come in and enjoy being with you. His desire is to have a relationship, not religion, with us. There is a huge difference.

Here is a prayer to pray out loud, as the Scripture says.

Dear Lord Jesus,

I know I am a sinner. I ask you to forgive me of my sins, and I invite you into my heart and to be my Lord and Savior. I thank you for dying on the cross and rising from the dead for me. Be my Lord and Savior.

I pray this in Jesus' Name.

To find out more, visit www.perryhall.life/destination

Author's Note

I pray first and foremost that you have made Jesus Lord of your life. This is the most important thing you will ever do. This will determine how you will spend eternity. I pray that you will now find a church to connect with and begin to grow. I pray that you will continue to want more and more of Jesus. I pray that people will see what you have and want to have it as well. I pray that you will share Christ with everyone you know because their eternity depends on it.

God bless you,

Dom

Website: www.perryhall.life

Like us on Facebook: www.facebook.com/phfwc

Watch services online: www.perryhall.life/live